This book belongs to:

_____

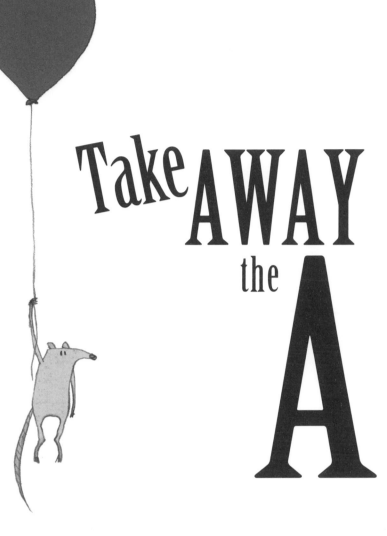

Take AWAY the A

First published in Great Britain in 2015 by Andersen Press Ltd.,
20 Vauxhall Bridge Road, London SW1V 2SA.
Originally published by Enchanted Lion Books, 351 Van Brunt Street,
Brooklyn, NY 11231, USA
Copyright © 2014, Enchanted Lion Books
Text copyright © 2014 by Michaël Escoffier
Illustrations copyright © 2014 by Kris Di Giacomo
Translation arranged through VeroK Agency, Barcelona, Spain
Printed and bound in China.

10   9   8   7   6   5   4   3   2   1

British Library Cataloguing in Publication Data available.

ISBN 978 1 78344 344 4

Take AWAY the A

By Michaël Escoffier

Illustrated by Kris Di Giacomo

An ALPHABEAST of a book!

Andersen Press

Without the

A

the BEAST is the BEST.

Without the

B

the BRIDE
goes for
a RIDE

Without
the

the CHAIR has HAIR.

Without the

D

DICE are ICE.

Without the

E

BEARS stay
behind BARS.

Without the

F

the SCARF
hides a SCAR.

Without
the

G

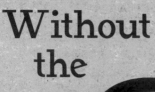

the GLOVE
falls in LOVE.

Without the

H

THREE
climb a
TREE.

Without
the

I

STAIRS
lead to the
STARS.

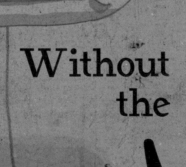

Without the **J**

Without the

K

Without the

L

PLANTS
hide their
PANTS.

Without the **M**

the **FARM** is too **FAR**.

the MOON says MOO!

Without the **O**

FOUR wear FUR.

Without the

P

the PLATE
is too LATE.

Without the **Q**

the FAQIR
goes to the FAIR.

the CRAB
hails a CAB.

Without the S

SNOW falls NOW.

BOATS carry BOAS.

Without the

U

my AUNT
is an ANT.

Without the **V**

SEVEN are SEEN.

Without
the

W

the WITCH
has an ITCH.

Without
the

FOXES
are
FOES.

Without the
Y

YOURS is OURS.

Without the

our alphabet cannot be said!

BEAST STAIRS
BRIDE JAM
CHAIR
DICE MONKEY
PLANTS
BEARS FARM
SCARF
GLOVE MOON
THREE FOUR